MW00568983

30 PARTY CAKES

Imaginative cakes for every celebration

This edition published in 1996 by
Smithmark Publishers, a division of U.S. Media Holdings Inc.
16 East 32nd Street, New York, NY 10016

Smithmark books are available for bulk purchase and for sales
promotion and for premium use.
For details write or call the Manager of Special Sales, Smithmark
Publishers, 16 East 32nd Street, New York, NY 10016; (212 532-6600)

© 1996 Anness Publishing Limited

All rights reserved. No part of this publication may be reproduced,
stored in a retrieval system, or transmitted in any way or by any means,
electronic, mechanical, photocopying, recording or otherwise,
without the prior written permission of the copyright holder.

Produced by
Anness Publishing Limited
1 Boundary Row
London SE1 8HP

Printed and bound in China

10 9 8 7 6 5 4 3 2 1

CONTENTS

INTRODUCTION

There is nothing to beat the look of disbelief followed by unsurpassed joy that comes over the face of a child (or adult) when presented with a special cake as the finale to a party. What better excuse for making a cake than a party or celebration – large or small. Whether it's a Party Teddy cake for baby's first birthday or the big White Chocolate Celebration Cake for a large family gathering, you will find something in this book for every occasion.

Cake decorating is a fascinating and rewarding craft and it is easier than you may think to create simple, effective novelty cakes. Every recipe in the book takes you from baking the basic cake, filling, icing and through to the final decorating. If you are a beginner the easy-to-follow instructions will guide you every step of the way. A more experienced cake maker can of course adapt the designs to suit, changing colour schemes, using different piping techniques and so on.

When making novelty cakes it is wise to allow plenty of time for adequate preparation. To ensure that you have a well-shaped cake to use as a base, it is important to line the cake tin as instructed. Although it may seem tedious, it is heart-breaking to have a cake stick to a tin so that

it comes out misshapen. Why not cut out a few extra circles of paper to fit in your most-used tins and keep them handy in a drawer? Use a non-flavoured oil, such as sunflower, for greasing to save melting fat.

Always have all the ingredients at room temperature before baking. To make things even more simple some ingredients can be bought ready-prepared, such as chopped and toasted nuts. Purchased marzipan and sugarpaste (fondant) icing are a boon – they are also easier for a beginner to handle as they are not as soft as the home-made variety.

Piping icing and shaping marzipan does take a little practice so be patient. Try an experimental row of icing on an upturned cake tin or plate before decorating the actual cake. Choose the simple designs for your first attempts and then as you gain in skill and confidence you will be able to tackle the more elaborate designs.

There are always occasions in your life when you may like to turn your hand to making and decorating a special celebration cake, so look through the following pages where you will be sure to find an appropriate design. Enjoy baking and decorating a cake for that special person and don't worry if it isn't totally perfect – the time, thought and love that have gone into its making will be more than appreciated by the lucky recipient.

St Clement's Marbled Crown

A tangy orange and lemon marbled cake is transformed into a spectacular centrepiece by the pretty arrangement of fresh flowers in the centre of the ring.

Ingredients

Serves 8

175 g/6 oz/¾ cup butter
75 g/3 oz/½ cup light soft
brown sugar
3 eggs, separated
grated rind and juice 1 orange
165 g/5½ oz/1⅓ cups
self-raising flour
75 g/3 oz/6 tbsp caster
(superfine) sugar
grated rind and juice of 1 lemon
15 g/½ oz/2 tbsp ground almonds
350 ml/12 fl oz/1½ cups double
(heavy) cream
1 tbsp Grand Marnier

To Decorate

16 crystallized (candied) orange and
lemon slices
silver dragées
8 gold sugared almonds
fresh flowers

Storing

Best eaten the day of making.

1 Preheat the oven to 180°C/350°F/ Gas 4. Grease and flour a 900 ml/1½ pint/3¾ cup ring mould. To make the orange cake, cream half the butter and the soft brown sugar together until the mixture is light and fluffy. Gradually beat in the egg yolks, orange rind and juice and fold in 75 g/3 oz/¾ cup of the flour. To make the lemon cake, cream the remaining butter and the caster (superfine) sugar together, stir in the lemon rind and juice and fold in the remaining flour along with the ground almonds. Whisk the egg whites until they form stiff peaks, then fold them gently into the cake mixture.

3 Whip the cream and Grand Marnier together until thick. Using a large palette knife (metal spatula), spread the cream over the cooled cake in large swirls.

2 Spoon the mixtures alternately into the tin. Using a skewer, swirl through the mixture, to create a marble effect. Bake in the oven for 45–50 minutes, or until a skewer inserted into the cake comes out clean. Cool for 10 minutes and turn on to a wire rack to cool completely.

4 Decorate the ring with the crystallized (candied) fruits, dragées and almonds to resemble a jewelled crown. Arrange a few pretty, fresh flowers in the centre.

CHOCOLATE GATEAU TERRINE

A spectacular finale to a special occasion meal. You'll find this is well worth the time and effort to make.

INGREDIENTS

SERVES 10–12

115 g/4 oz/½ cup butter, softened
few drops of vanilla essence (extract)
115 g/4 oz/½ cup (superfine) caster sugar
2 eggs
115 g/4 oz/1 cup self-raising flour
50 ml/2 fl oz/¼ cup milk
25 g/1 oz/½ cup desiccated (shredded) coconut and bud roses to decorate

FOR THE LIGHT CHOCOLATE FILLING
115 g/4 oz/½ cup butter, softened
2 tbsp icing (confectioner's) sugar, sifted
75 g/3 oz plain (semi-sweet) chocolate, melted
250 ml/8 fl oz/1 cup double (heavy) cream, lightly whipped

FOR THE DARK CHOCOLATE FILLING
115 g/4 oz plain chocolate, chopped
115 g/4 oz/½ cup butter
2 eggs
2 tbsp caster (superfine) sugar
250 ml/8 fl oz/1 cup double cream, lightly whipped
50 g/2 oz/½ cup cocoa powder, sifted
2 tbsp gelatine powder dissolved in 2 tbsp hot water

FOR THE WHITE CHOCOLATE TOPPING
225 g/8 oz white chocolate
115 g/4 oz/½ cup butter

1 Preheat the oven to 180°/350°F/ Gas 4. Grease a 900 g/2 lb loaf tin, line the base and sides with greaseproof (wax) paper and grease the paper. To make the cake, beat the butter, vanilla and sugar together until light and fluffy. Add the eggs, 1 at a time, beating well. Fold in the flour and milk. Put in the tin and bake for 25–30 minutes. Leave for 5 minutes, then turn on to a wire rack, peel off the lining paper and leave to cool completely.

3 Line the loaf tin with clear film (plastic wrap), allowing plenty to hang over the edges. Cut the cake horizontally into three layers. Spread two of the layers with light chocolate filling, then place 1 of them, filling side up, in the base of the tin. Cover with half the dark chocolate filling. Chill for 10 minutes. Repeat with remaining cake and fillings. Top with the last layer of cake and chill again.

2 To make the light chocolate filling, beat together the butter and icing (confectioner's) sugar until creamy. Add the chocolate and cream and mix well. Cover and chill. To make the dark chocolate filling, melt the chocolate and butter very gently in a pan. Cool. Whisk the eggs and sugar together until thick and frothy. Fold in the cream, cocoa, dissolved gelatine and chocolate until evenly blended.

4 To make the white chocolate topping, melt the chocolate and butter very gently in a small pan. Cool slightly. Turn the terrine out on to a wire rack, removing the clear film. Trim the edges and pour over the topping, spreading evenly over the sides. Sprinkle the coconut over the top and sides. When set, put on a plate and decorate with roses.

EASTER SPONGE CAKE

This light lemon sponge cake is decorated with lemon butter icing and marzipan flowers.

SERVES 10–12
3-egg quantity lemon-flavoured
quick mix sponge
2 quantities lemon-flavoured
butter icing
50 g/2 oz/½ cup flaked almonds,
toasted
50 g/2 oz white marzipan
green, orange and yellow food
colourings

TO DECORATE
10 green cut-out marzipan flowers
8 orange cut-out marzipan flowers
6 cut-out marzipan daffodils

STORING
*Stored in a container in the
refrigerator the cake will keep fresh
for up to 3 days.*

1 Preheat the oven to 160°/325°F/
Gas 3. Grease 2 x 20 cm/8 in
round sandwich tins (layer cake
pans), and line the bases with
greased greaseproof (waxed) paper.
Divided the sponge mixture between
the tins and bake for 35–40 minutes
until the tops spring back when
lightly pressed. Turn the cakes out,
remove the lining paper and cool on
a wire rack.

2 Sandwich the cakes together
with one-quarter of the icing.
Spread two-thirds of the icing on the
top and sides, making lines on the
top. Press almonds on to the sides.

3 Place the remaining icing in a
piping bag fitted with a star
nozzle and pipe a scroll edging. Using
the marzipan and food colourings,
make the cut-out marzipan flowers.
Arrange the marzipan flowers on the
cake and leave the icing to set.

EXOTIC CELEBRATION GATEAU

Use any tropical fruits you can find to make a spectacular display of colours and tastes.

INGREDIENTS

SERVES 8–10

175 g/6 oz/¾ cup butter, softened
175 g/6 oz/¾ cup caster (superfine) sugar
3 eggs, beaten
250 g/9 oz/2¼ cups self-raising flour
2–3 tbsp milk
6–8 tbsp light rum
450 ml/¾ pint/1¾ cups double (heavy) cream
25 g/1 oz/¼ cup icing (confectioner's) sugar, sifted

TO DECORATE

450 g/1 lb mixed fresh exotic and soft fruits, such as figs, star fruit, etc.
6 tbsp apricot jam, warmed and sieved
2 tbsp warm water
sifted icing (confectioner's) sugar

STORING

This cake will keep for up to 2 days in the refrigerator.

1 Preheat the oven to 190°/375°F/ Gas 5. Grease and flour a deep 20 cm/8 in ring mould. Beat the butter and sugar together until light and fluffy. Gradually beat in the eggs, then fold in the flour and milk. Spoon into the prepared tin. Bake in the oven for 40–45 minutes. Turn out on to a wire rack and cool.

2 Place the cake on a serving plate, then prick all over with a skewer. Drizzle over the rum.

3 Whip together the cream and icing (confectioner's) sugar and use to cover the cake. Arrange the fruits on the cake and brush them with a mixture of jam and water. Sift over a little icing sugar to finish.

CHOCOLATE AND FRESH CHERRY GATEAU

The addition of spices to this attractive gâteau adds an exotic kick.
A compote of fresh cherries fills the hollowed-out centre and the cake is
coated with a rich chocolate icing.

INGREDIENTS

SERVES 8
115 g/4 oz/½ cup butter
150 g/5 oz/⅔ cup caster
(superfine) sugar
3 eggs, lightly beaten
175 g/6 oz/1 cup plain (semi-sweet)
chocolate chips, melted
4 tbsp Kirsch
150 g/5 oz/1¼ cups self-raising flour
1 tsp ground cinnamon
½ tsp ground cloves
350 g/12 oz fresh cherries, stoned
(pitted) and halved
3 tbsp Morello cherry jam
1 tsp lemon juice

FOR THE FROSTING
115 g/4 oz/¼ cup plain (semi-sweet)
chocolate chips
50 g/2 oz/¼ cup unsalted (sweet)
butter
4 tbsp double (heavy) cream

TO DECORATE
75 g/3 oz/½ cup white
chocolate chips
14–18 fresh cherries
a few rose leaves, washed and dried

STORING
Place in an airtight container and keep
in the refrigerator for up to 2 days.

1 Preheat the oven to 160°/325°F/ Gas 3. Grease a 20 cm/8 in springform tin and line the base with greased greaseproof (wax) paper. Cream the butter and 115 g/4 oz/ ½ cup of sugar together. Gradually beat in the eggs. Stir in the melted chocolate and 2 tbsp of the Kirsch. Sift the flour and spices together and fold into the creamed mixture. Put in the prepared tin and bake for 55–60 minutes or until a skewer inserted in the centre comes out clean. Remove from the oven, cool in the tin for 10 minutes. Turn out on to a wire rack and cool.

2 Place the cherries, remaining Kirsch and sugar in a small pan. Heat gently to dissolve the sugar, cover and simmer for 10 minutes, then simmer uncovered for 10 minutes, until the mixture is thick. Leave to cool.

3 Cut the cake in half. Using a 15 cm/6 in saucer as a template, cut out a circle, 1 cm/½ in deep, from the centre of 1 sponge. Crumble into the cherry mixture and stir. Use to fill the hollowed cake. Smooth the surface and cover with the top half of cake. Boil the jam and lemon juice for 1 minute, and brush over the cake.

4 To make the frosting, melt the chocolate, butter and cream in a small pan. Cool until the mixture thickens. Pour over the cake, to completely cover the top and sides. Leave to set.

5 Melt the white chocolate chips in a bowl over a pan of hot water. Dip each cherry halfway into the chocolate and leave to set on non-stick paper (baking parchment). Using a paintbrush, coat the underside of the rose leaves with a thick layer of the remaining chocolate. Leave to set on non-stick paper. When set, carefully peel away the leaves. Decorate the cake with cherries and chocolate leaves.

GOLDEN WEDDING HEART CAKE

*Creamy gold colours, delicate frills and dainty iced blossoms give this
cake a special celebratory appeal.*

INGREDIENTS

SERVES 30
23 cm/9 in round rich fruit cake
4 tbsp apricot jam, warmed and sieved
900 g/2 lb marzipan
900 g/2 lb sugarpaste (fondant) icing
cream food colouring
115 g/4 oz/⅓ quantity royal icing

TO DECORATE
stamens
foil-wrapped chocolate hearts

STORING
*The finished cake can be kept for up
to 3 months in an airtight container.*

1 Brush the cake with the jam.
Roll out the marzipan and use
to cover the cake. Leave to dry.

2 Colour 675 g/1½ lb of the
sugarpaste (fondant) very pale
cream. Brush the marzipan with a
little water, roll out the sugarpaste
and use to cover the cake. Put the
cake on a cake board. Using a
crimping tool carefully crimp the top
edge of the cake.

3 Mark the top circumference of
the cake evenly into eight and
crimp evenly spaced slanting lines
around the side, from the top to the
bottom edges. Using a heart-shaped
plunger tool, emboss the edge of the
cake. Place a 7.5 cm/3 in plain
biscuit cutter in the centre of the
cake and use as a guide to emboss
hearts in a circle.

5 To make the frills, roll out the
reserved sugarpaste thinly. Using
a frill cutter, cut out two rings from
each colour. With the end of a
wooden cocktail stick roll firmly
back and forth around the edge until
it becomes thinner and begins to frill.
Repeat with remaining rings. Cut
each ring in half to make 2 frills.

4 Colour half the remaining
sugarpaste cream and the other
half pale cream. Wrap half of each
colour in clear film (plastic wrap).
Roll out and use blossom cutters to
cut out large and small flowers. Make
a pin hole in the centre of each large
flower. Leave to dry. Pipe royal icing
on to the stamens and thread through
each large flower. Allow to dry.

6 Using a little water, attach the
frills in alternate shades next to
the crimped lines on the side of the
cake. Crimp the edges of the deeper
coloured frills. Arrange the flowers
on the top and side of the cake,
securing with royal icing, and place
foil-wrapped chocolate hearts in the
centre of the cake.

HAZELNUT CHOCOLATE
MERINGUE TORTE WITH PEARS

Do not assemble this torte more than 3–4 hours before serving, as the
pears may give off liquid and soften the cream too much.

INGREDIENTS

SERVES 8–10

150 g/5 oz/¾ cup granulated sugar
1 vanilla pod, split
475 ml/16 fl oz/2 cups water
2 ripe pears, peeled, halved and cored
2 tbsp pear or hazelnut-flavour liqueur
6 egg whites
pinch of salt
350 g/12 oz/2½ cups icing
(confectioner's) sugar
185 g/6½ oz/1¼ cups hazelnuts,
toasted and medium ground
1 tsp vanilla essence (extract)
50 g/1 oz plain (semi-sweet) chocolate,
melted

FOR THE CHOCOLATE CREAM

275 g/10 oz fine quality bittersweet or
plain (semi-sweet) chocolate, chopped
475 ml/16 fl oz/2 cups whipping or
double (heavy) cream
65 ml/2 fl oz/¼ cup pear or
hazelnut-flavour liqueur

STORING

This cake does not keep and should be
eaten within 4 hours of assembling.

1 In a pan large enough to hold the pears in a single layer combine sugar, vanilla pod and water. Bring to the boil, stirring until the sugar dissolves. Reduce the heat and lower the pears into the syrup. Cover and simmer gently for 12–15 minutes until tender. Remove from the heat and allow the pears to cool in the liquid. Remove the pears and dry gently with kitchen paper (paper towels). Sprinkle with the liqueur, cover and chill.

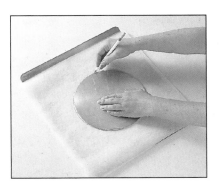

2 Preheat the oven to 180°C/350°F/ Gas 4. Draw a 23 cm/9 in circle in the centre of each of two sheets of non-stick paper (baking parchment), and invert on to baking sheets. Beat the egg whites until frothy. Add the salt and whisk until soft peaks form. Gradually add the sugar, beating well after each addition until the meringue is stiff and glossy. Gently fold in the nuts and vanilla and spoon the meringue on to the circles marked on the paper, smoothing the tops and sides. Bake for 1 hour until dry and firm. Turn off the oven and allow to cool in the oven for 2–3 hours or until completely dry.

3 Melt the chocolate in a bowl over a pan of hot water. Cool the chocolate to room temperature. Whisk the cream until it holds soft peaks. Quickly fold in the cream and the liqueur. Spoon one-third of the chocolate cream into a piping bag fitted with a star nozzle.

4 Using a sharp knife, thinly slice each pear half lengthways. Place 1 meringue layer on a plate. Spread with half the chocolate cream and arrange half the sliced pears evenly over the cream. Pipe a border of rosettes around the edge. Top with the second meringue and spread with the remaining chocolate cream. Arrange the remaining pear slices attractively on top. Pipe a border of rosettes around the edge. Drizzle the melted chocolate over the pears. Chill well before serving.

WHITE CHOCOLATE CELEBRATION CAKE

The ingredients for the cake mixture make 1 x 30 cm/12 in cake. You will need to double the ingredients for the cake, preparing each batch separately to ensure even baking. If you wish to make a smaller cake, bake only 1 layer, and split and fill with half quantities of lemon syrup, lemon curd and buttercream.

INGREDIENTS

SERVES 40–50. MAKES 1 LAYER
600 g/1 lb 5 oz/4 cups plain
(all-purpose) flour
2 tsp bicarbonate of soda
(baking soda)
pinch of salt
225 g/8 oz white chocolate, chopped
250 ml/8 fl oz/1 cup whipping
or double (heavy) cream
225 g/8 oz/1 cup unsalted (sweet)
butter, softened
400 g/14 oz/2 cups caster
(superfine) sugar
6 eggs
2 tsp lemon essence (extract)
grated rind of 1 lemon
325 ml/11 fl oz/1⅓ cups buttermilk
2 x 500 g/1¼ lb jars lemon curd
50–115 g/2–4 oz/4–8 tbsp unsalted
(sweet) butter or margarine, softened
chocolate leaves, to decorate
fresh flowers, to decorate

FOR THE LEMON SYRUP
90 g/3½ oz/½ cup granulated sugar
120 ml/4 fl oz/½ cup water
2 tbsp fresh lemon juice

FOR THE WHITE CHOCOLATE CREAM
CHEESE BUTTERCREAM
700 g/1 lb 9 oz white chocolate,
chopped
1 kg/2¼ lb cream cheese, softened
500 g/1¼ lb/2½ cups unsalted (sweet)
butter, at room temperature
4 tbsp fresh lemon juice
1 tsp lemon essence (extract)

1 Prepare the cake layers. Preheat the oven to 180°/350°F/Gas 4. Grease a 30 cm/12 in cake or springform tin. Line base with non-stick baking paper (baking parchment), grease again, then flour lightly. Sift together the flour, bicarbonate of soda (baking soda) and salt. In a pan gently melt the chocolate and cream, stirring until smooth. Cool. Beat the butter until creamy, then add the sugar and beat for 2–3 minutes. Beat in the eggs. Slowly beat in the melted chocolate, lemon essence (extract) and rind. Stir in the flour and buttermilk in alternate batches until a smooth batter is formed. Pour into the tin. Bake for 1 hour or until a skewer comes out clean. Cool in the tin for 10 minutes then turn on to a wire rack and cool. Make a second cake in the same way.

2 To make the syrup, combine the sugar and water in a small saucepan. Bring to the boil, stirring until the sugar dissolves. Stir in the lemon juice and cool.

3 To make the buttercream, melt the chocolate in a bowl over a pan of hot water. Cool slightly. Beat the cheese until smooth. Gradually beat in the chocolate, butter, lemon juice and essence. Chill.

4 To assemble, split each cake in half. Spoon the syrup over each layer, allowing it to soak in, then repeat. Spread the bottom half of each cake with lemon curd and replace the top layers. Spread one quarter of the buttercream over the top of 1 of the filled cakes. Place the second filled cake on top. Spread softened butter over the top and sides to create a smooth, crumb-free surface. Chill.

5 Place the cake on a plate. Reserving one quarter of the buttercream spread the rest over the top and side of the cake. Pipe the reserved buttercream in a shell pattern around edges of the cake. Decorate with chocolate leaves and fresh flowers.

LUCKY HORSESHOE

This horseshoe-shaped cake, to wish "good luck", is made from a round cake and the horseshoe shape is then cut out. Horseshoe-shaped tins can be purchased or hired from cake decorating specialists.

INGREDIENTS

SERVES 30–35
25 cm/10 in round rich fruit cake
4 tbsp apricot jam, warmed and sieved
800 g/1¾ lb marzipan
1 kg/2¼ lb sugarpaste (fondant) icing
peach and blue food colourings
silver balls
115 g/4 oz/⅙ quantity royal icing

STORING
The cake can be kept for up to 3 months in an airtight container.

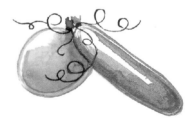

1 Draw a horseshoe shape on a sheet of greaseproof (wax) paper. Cut this shape out of the cake, using the template. Brush the cake with the apricot jam. Roll out 350 g/12 oz of the marzipan to a 25 cm/10 in circle. Using the template, cut out the shape and cover the top of the cake with the marzipan horseshoe.

2 Using string measure the circumference of the cake as far as the opening and the height of the side. Take the remaining marzipan and roll out for the side, using string as a guide. Use to cover the side. Using the same method and the trimmings, cover the inside of the horseshoe. Put the cake on a cake board and leave to dry.

3 Colour 800g/1¾ lb of the sugarpaste (fondant) peach. Brush the marzipan lightly with water and cover the cake in the same way as the marzipan.

4 Draw the design for the ribbon insertion on the horseshoe template. Cut 13 pieces of pale blue ribbon fractionally longer than the size of each slit. Place the template on the cake, and cut through the lines with a scalpel to make slits. With tweezers insert 1 end of the ribbon into the first slit and the other end into the second slit. Leave a space and repeat, filling all the slits with ribbon. Leave to dry.

5 Colour half the remaining sugarpaste pale blue and leave the rest white. Roll out the blue icing and, using a small horseshoe template, cut out 9 shapes. Mark small lines around the centre of each horseshoe. Cut out 12 large and 15 small blossoms with blossom cutters. Press a silver ball into the centres of the large blossoms. Repeat with the white icing. Decorate the cake with ribbon. Secure the horseshoes and blossom in place with royal icing.

FRENCH CHOCOLATE CAKE

This very dense chocolate cake can be made up to 3 days before serving,
but decorate with icing (confectioner's) sugar on the day it is to be served.

INGREDIENTS

SERVES 10
250 g/9 oz bittersweet chocolate,
chopped
225 g/8 oz/1 cup unsalted (sweet)
butter, cut into pieces
90 g/3½ oz/½ cup granulated sugar
2 tbsp brandy or orange-flavour
liqueur
4 eggs
1 tbsp plain flour
icing (confectioner's) sugar,
for dusting
whipped or soured cream, to serve

STORING
Store up to 3 days in a covered
container in the refrigerator.

1 Preheat the oven to 180°C/350°/
Gas 4. Grease a 23 cm/9 in
round springform tin, line the base
with non-stick paper (baking
parchment) and grease the paper.
Wrap the base and side of the tin
in foil to prevent water seeping in.
In a pan over a low heat, melt the
chocolate, butter and sugar, stirring
frequently until smooth; cool slightly.
Stir in the liqueur. Whisk the eggs
lightly for about 1 minute. Beat in
the flour then slowly beat in the
chocolate mixture until well blended.

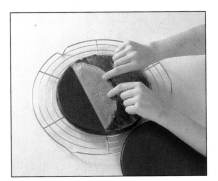

3 Remove the side of the
springform tin and turn the cake
on to a wire rack. Remove the base
and lining paper, so the bottom of
the cake is now the top.

2 Pour into the tin and place in a
roasting tin and pour in boiling
water to a depth of 2 cm/¾ in. Bake
for 25–30 minutes until the edge of
the cake is set, but the centre is still
soft. Remove the tin from the water
bath and remove the foil. Cool
completely (the cake may sink in the
centre and crack).

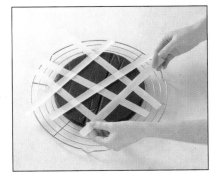

4 Cut 6–8 strips of non-stick
paper 2.5 cm/1 in wide and place
randomly over the cake. Dust with
icing (confectioner's) sugar, then
carefully remove the paper strips.
Slide the cake on to a plate and serve
with cream.

SWEETHEART

The heart-shaped run-outs can be prepared a week before the cake
is made to ensure that they are completely dry.

INGREDIENTS

SERVES 8–10
3-egg quantity quick mix sponge
⅓ quantity butter icing
3 tbsp apricot jam, warmed and sieved
450 g/1 lb marzipan
675 g/1½ lb sugarpaste (fondant) icing,
coloured pink
115 g/4 oz/⅙ quantity royal icing,
coloured red

1 Preheat the oven to 160°/325°/ Gas 3. Grease a 20 cm/8 in round cake tin, line the base with greaseproof (wax) paper and grease the paper. Spoon in the cake mixture and bake for 45–55 minutes or until a skewer inserted in the centre comes out clean. Cool for 5 minutes, then turn out on to a wire rack.

2 Remove the lining paper. Split and fill the cake with the butter icing. Put on a cake board and brush with the apricot jam. Cover with marzipan then a layer of pink sugarpaste (fondant), large enough to cover the cake and board. Smooth the surface and trim. Mark the edge with a spoon handle.

3 Draw heart shapes on non-stick paper (baking parchment) and using the red royal icing make heart-shaped run-outs (see Birthday Balloons). Leave to dry for 48 hours. Remove the hearts and arrange on the cake, place candles in the centre and tie ribbon around the side.

HEART ENGAGEMENT CAKES

*For a celebratory engagement party, these sumptuous cakes make
the perfect centrepiece.*

INGREDIENTS

SERVES 20
*4-egg quantity chocolate-flavour
quick mix sponge
350 g/12 oz plain
(semi-sweet) chocolate, melted
2 x quantity coffee-flavour butter icing
icing (confectioner's) sugar, for sifting
fresh raspberries, to decorate*

1 Preheat the oven to 160°/325°F/
Gas 3. Grease 2 x 20 cm/8 in
heart-shaped tins, line the bases with
greaseproof (wax) paper and grease
the paper. Put the cake mixture in
the tins and bake in the oven for
25–30 minutes or until firm to the
touch. Turn out on to a wire rack,
peel off the lining paper and cool.

2 Pour the chocolate on to a
smooth surface such as a marble
slab. Spread out and leave until just
set, but not hard. To make the curls,
hold a large sharp knife at an angle
to the chocolate and push it along in
short sawing movements.

3 Cut each cake in half and use
one-third of the butter icing to
fill both cakes. Use the remaining
icing to coat the tops and sides of
the cakes. Place the cakes on cake
boards. Cover the tops and sides
with the chocolate curls. Sift a little
icing (confectioner's) sugar over the
top and decorate with raspberries.
Chill until ready to serve.

ICED PRALINE TORTE

Make this elaborate torte several days ahead, decorate it and return it to the
freezer. Allow the torte to stand at room temperature for an hour before serving.

INGREDIENTS

SERVES 8

115 g/4 oz/1 cup almonds or hazelnuts
115 g/4 oz/8 tbsp caster
(superfine) sugar
115 g/4 oz/⅔ cup raisins
6 tbsp rum or brandy
115 g/4 oz plain (semi-sweet)
chocolate broken into squares
2 tbsp milk
450 ml/¾ pint/
1¼ cups double (heavy) cream
2 tbsp strong black coffee
16 sponge fingers (ladyfingers)

TO DECORATE

150 ml/¼ pint/⅔ cup double (heavy)
cream, whipped
50 g/2 oz/½ cup flaked almonds,
toasted
15 g/½ oz plain chocolate, melted

STORING

Keep in the freezer for up to 2 weeks.

1 Lightly oil a baking (cookie) sheet. Put the nuts and sugar into a heavy-based pan and heat gently until the sugar melts. Swirl the pan to coat the nuts. Cook slowly until the sugar caramelizes. This will only take a few minutes. Pour on to the baking sheet and leave to cool completely. Then grind to a powder in a blender or food processor.

2 Soak the raisins in 3 tbsp of the rum or brandy for at least 1 hour. Melt the chocolate and milk in a bowl over a pan of hot water. Remove and cool. Lightly grease a 1.2 litre/2 pint/5 cup loaf tin and line with greaseproof (wax) paper. Whisk the cream until it holds soft peaks. Whisk in the cooled chocolate. Fold in the praline and the soaked raisins, with any liquid.

3 Mix the coffee and remaining rum or brandy in a shallow dish. Dip in the sponge fingers (ladyfingers) and arrange half in the base of the tin. Cover with the chocolate mixture and add another layer of soaked sponge fingers. Freeze overnight. Dip the tin briefly into warm water and turn the torte out on to a plate. Cover with whipped cream. Sprinkle the top with the almonds and drizzle with melted chocolate.

DAISY CHRISTENING CAKE

*A ring of moulded daisies sets off this pretty pink christening cake.
It can be made in easy stages, giving time for the various icings to dry
before adding the next layer.*

INGREDIENTS

SERVES 20–25
20 cm/8 in round rich fruit cake
3 tbsp apricot jam, warmed and sieved
675 g/1½ lb marzipan
900 g/2 lb/1½ quantity royal icing
115 g/4 oz sugarpaste (fondant) icing
pink and yellow food colourings

STORING
*This cake can be kept for up to
3 months in an airtight container.*

1 Brush the cake with the apricot jam. Roll out the marzipan and use to cover the cake. Leave to dry. Place the cake on a cake board. Colour three-quarters of the royal icing pink. Flat ice the cake with 3 or 4 layers of smooth icing, using the white icing for the top and the pink for the side. Allow each layer to dry overnight. Set aside a little of both icings in airtight containers.

2 To make the daisies cut off a small piece of sugarpaste (fondant). Dust your fingers with a little cornflour (cornstarch). Shape the icing with your fingers to look like a golf tee, with a stem and a thin, flat, round top.

4 For the plaque, cut out a 5 cm/2 in fluted sugarpaste round. Frill the edge with a cocktail stick (toothpick). Leave to dry. Paint the name and edge in pink.

3 Using scissors, make small cuts all the way around the edge of the daisy. Curl the cut edges slightly. Make 28 daisies and place on a sheet of greaseproof (wax) paper to dry. Trim the stems and paint the edges pink and the centres yellow.

5 Pipe white royal icing in a twisted rope around the edges of the cake. Pipe stars around the top of the cake with pink royal icing. Attach the plaque and daisies with royal icing and decorate with ribbons.

FIRE ENGINE

This jolly fire engine is simplicity itself as the decorations are mainly bought sweets and novelties.

INGREDIENTS

SERVES 16
4-egg quantity quick mix sponge
⅓ quantity butter icing
4 tbsp apricot jam, warmed and sieved
350 g/12 oz marzipan
350 g/12 oz sugarpaste (fondant) icing,
coloured red
liquorice strips
115 g/4 oz/⅙ quantity royal icing
black and green food colourings
115 g/4 oz sugarpaste icing
sweets
2 silver bells
50 g/2 oz/1 cup desiccated (shredded)
coconut

STORING
This cake will keep for 1 week loosely covered in a cool, dry place.

1 Preheat the oven to 160°/325°F/ Gas 3. Grease a 20 cm/8 in square cake tin, line the base with greaseproof (wax) paper and grease the paper. Spoon in the cake mixture and bake in the oven for about 50–60 minutes or until a skewer inserted in the centre comes out clean. Leave in the tin for 5 minutes, then turn out on to a wire rack. Remove the lining paper and cool.

2 Split and fill the cake with butter icing. Cut in half and place one half on top of the other.

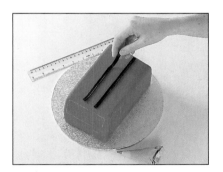

3 Place on a cake board and brush with apricot jam. Trim a thin wedge off the front edge to make a sloping windscreen. Cover with a layer of marzipan and red sugarpaste (fondant) icing. Mark the windows, ladder and wheels.

4 Use the liquorice strips to make the ladder. Colour half the royal icing black and use some to stick the ladder to the top. Roll out the white sugarpaste, cut out and stick on the windows with water.

5 Pipe round the windows in black royal icing. Stick on sweets for headlights, lamps and wheels and stick the silver bells on the roof. Colour the coconut green. Spread royal icing over the board and sprinkle with coconut. Stick sweets to the board and press in candles.

DRUM

This is a colourful cake for very young children. The ropes can be made by rolling by hand on a smooth work surface, but a perspex smoother gives a much better result.

INGREDIENTS

SERVES 6–8
2-egg quantity quick mix sponge
⅛ quantity butter icing
2 tbsp apricot jam, warmed and sieved
350 g/12 oz marzipan
450 g/1 lb sugarpaste (fondant) icing
red, blue and yellow food colourings

STORING
This cake will keep for 1 week loosely
covered in a cool, dry place.

1   Preheat the oven to 160°C/325°F/ Gas 3. Grease a 15 cm/6 in round cake tin, line with greaseproof (wax) paper and grease the paper. Spoon in the cake mixture and bake in the oven for 35–45 minutes or until a skewer inserted into the centre comes out clean. Leave in the tin for 5 minutes, then turn out on to a wire rack. Remove lining paper and cool. Split and fill the cake with butter icing. Brush with the jam.

2   Cover with marzipan and leave to dry. Colour half the sugarpaste (fondant) red. Roll out a strip and stick to the side of the cake with water.

3   Roll out a circle of white sugarpaste to fit the top and divide the rest in half. Colour one half blue and the other yellow. Roll the blue into two long sausages and stick around the base and top of the cake with water.

4   Mark the cake into six around the top and bottom. Roll the yellow fondant into thin sausages and stick on the side of the cake as drum strings. Roll the remaining yellow fondant into 12 balls and stick where the strings join the drum.

5   Knead together red and white fondant until streaky and roll two balls and sticks. Dry overnight. Stick together with royal icing and place on the drum.

Birthday Balloons

A colourful cake for a child's birthday party, made using either a round sponge cake or fruit cake base.

Ingredients

Serves 8–20

20 cm/8 in round fruit cake or sponge, made using 4-egg quantity quick mix sponge
4 tbsp apricot jam, warmed and sieved
800 g/1¾ lb marzipan
900 g/2 lb sugarpaste (fondant) icing
red, green and yellow food colourings
cornflour (cornstarch), for dusting
3 eggs
2 egg whites
450 g/1 lb/4 cups icing (confectioner's) sugar

Storing

The iced cake will keep well in a cool place for up to 3 weeks.

1 Place the cake on a cake board. Brush with apricot jam and cover with the marzipan. Colour 50 g/2 oz of the sugarpaste (fondant) red, 50 g/2 oz green and 115 g/4 oz yellow. Roll out the remaining icing on a surface dusted with cornflour (cornstarch) and use to cover the cake. Use 50 g/2 oz of the yellow icing to cover the cake board. With the tip of a skewer make a small hole in the pointed end of each egg. Empty the eggs into a bowl. Carefully wash and dry the empty egg shells.

3 Trace 16 balloon shapes on to a sheet of non-stick paper (baking parchment). Beat the egg whites with the icing (confectioner's) sugar until smooth and divide into four. Leaving one bowl white, add red, green and yellow colourings to each of the others. Place the white icing in a piping bag with a plain nozzle and pipe the balloon outlines. Thin the green icing with water to pouring consistency. Put in a piping bag with a plain nozzle and fill a third of the balloon shapes. Repeat with the red and yellow icings. Leave for 24 hours to dry.

2 Roll each icing out to a circle and use to cover the egg shells. Push a bamboo skewer through the hole and rest in a tall glass. Roll out the trimmings and cut out small stars from each colour. Dampen then secure to the bases of the balloons.

4 Carefully remove the balloons and attach to the sides of the cake with a little icing. Pipe balloon strings with white icing. Insert the large balloons into the cake and decorate with ribbon and candles.

Bella Bunny

This is a simple cake for very young children. The icing is spread over the cake and does not require any special techniques

Serves 6–8
4-egg quantity quick mix sponge
4 tbsp apricot jam, warmed and sieved
1 quantity butter icing
115 g/4 oz/2 cups dessicated (shredded) coconut
50 g/2 oz sugarpaste (fondant) icing
red and brown food colouring

1 Preheat the oven to 160°/325°F/ Gas 3. Grease 2 x 15 cm/6 in round cake tins, then line with greaseproof (wax) paper and grease the paper. Spoon in the cake mixture and bake for 35–45 minutes or until firm to the touch. Leave in the tins for 5 minutes, then turn out on to a wire rack. Remove the lining paper and leave to cool.

2 Split and fill the cakes with a little butter icing. Cut a 10 cm/4 in circle out of one cake and place both cakes on a cake board.

3 Use the trimmings to make the ears and feet. Brush with the jam. Cover with butter icing and press on the coconut. Colour one piece of sugarpaste (fondant) pink and one piece brown. Shape the nose, ears and eyes and put in place. Use cocktail sticks (toothpicks) for whiskers. Place marshmallows stuck with candles around the cake.

PARTY TEDDY

There is very little piping on this cake. The teddy is built up with
royal icing and coloured coconut.

INGREDIENTS

SERVES 16
4-egg quantity quick mix sponge
⅓ quantity butter icing
3 tbsp apricot jam, warmed and sieved
450 g/1 lb marzipan
350 g/12 oz sugarpaste (fondant) icing
25 g/1 oz/⅓ cup desiccated (shredded)
coconut
blue and black food colourings
115 g/4 oz/⅙ quantity royal icing

1 Preheat the oven to 160°C/325°F/
Gas 3. Grease a 20 cm/8 in
square cake tin, line with greaseproof
(waxed) paper and grease the paper.
Spoon in the cake mixture and bake
in the oven for 50–60 minutes or
until a skewer inserted in the centre
comes out clean. Leave in the tin for
5 minutes, then turn out on to a wire
rack. Remove the lining paper and
allow to cool.

2 Split and fill the cake with
butter icing. Place on a cake
board and brush with apricot jam.
Cover with marzipan then sugarpaste
(fondant). Leave to dry. Using a
template, carefully mark the position
of the teddy on the cake. Colour the
coconut blue.

3 Spread a thin layer of royal icing
over the teddy shape and quickly
sprinkle on the coconut. Roll out the
sugarpaste trimmings and cut out
nose, ears and paws. Stick on with
royal icing. Tie a ribbon around the
cake. Pipe on eyes, nose and mouth
with black royal icing, and a white
royal icing border around the base.

STRAWBERRY CAKE

A summer-time cake or for someone who's simply mad about strawberries!

INGREDIENTS

SERVES 10–12
3-egg quantity quick mix sponge
650 g/1 lb 7 oz marzipan
6 tbsp apricot jam, warmed and sieved
green, red and yellow food colourings
caster (superfine) sugar, to dredge

STORING
The finished cake can be kept in a cool, dry place for up to 2 days.

1 Preheat the oven to 180°/350°F/ Gas 4. Grease a 900 g/2 lb heart-shaped tin, line the base with greaseproof (wax) paper and grease the paper. Spoon in the cake mixture and bake in the oven for 35–40 minutes or until a skewer inserted in the centre comes out clean. Leave in the tin for 5 minutes, then turn out on to a wire rack, peel off the lining paper and leave to cool completely.

2 Colour 175 g/6 oz of the marzipan green. Brush a cake board with apricot jam. Roll out the green marzipan and cover the board.

3 Brush the remaining jam over the cake. Position the cake on the cake board. Colour 275 g/10 oz of marzipan red. Roll out to 5 mm/ ¼ in thick and use to cover the cake, smoothing down the sides. Trim. Use the handle of a teaspoon to indent the strawberry evenly all over.

4 To make the stalk, colour 175 g/6 oz of marzipan bright green. Cut in half and roll out one piece into a 10 x 15 cm/4 x 6 in rectangle. Cut "V" shapes along one long edge, leaving a border across the top. Roll up lightly and place on the cake, curling the leaves. Roll the other half of the marzipan into a sausage shape, bend it slightly, and place on the calyx to form the stalk.

5 Colour the remaining marzipan yellow. Pull off tiny pieces the size of an apple pip and roll into tear-shaped seeds. Place in the indentations all over the strawberry. Dust the cake with sifted caster (superfine) sugar.

JACK-IN-A-BOX

For a change, tiny edible flowers or letters can be stuck on to the sides of the box.

INGREDIENTS

SERVES 6–8
3-egg quantity quick mix sponge
⅙ quantity butter icing
3 tbsp apricot jam, warmed and sieved
350 g/12 oz marzipan
450 g/1 lb sugarpaste (fondant) icing
ice cream cornet
115 g/4 oz /⅙ quantity royal icing
blue, black, green, red and yellow
food colourings
silver balls

STORING
This cake will keep for 1 week
loosely covered in a cool, dry place.

1 Preheat the oven to 160°C/325°F
Gas 3. Grease a 15 cm/6 in
square tin, line the base with
greaseproof (wax) paper and grease
the paper. Spoon in the cake mixture
and bake for 45–55 minutes or until
a skewer inserted in the centre comes
out clean. Leave in the tin for
5 minutes, then turn out on to a wire
rack. Remove the lining paper and
leave to cool.

3 Sandwich the rectangles together
on top of the large square to
make a cube. Place on a cake board
and brush with apricot jam. Cover
with marzipan then sugarpaste
(fondant). Shape the remaining cube
of cake into a ball for the head.
Brush with jam and cover with
marzipan then sugarpaste.

4 Cut the top off the ice cream
cornet. Stick the wide part in the
centre of the cake with royal icing
then stick the head on top. Colour a
small piece of sugarpaste blue, roll
out and cut a fluted circle with a
small inner circle. Cut one side, open
out then roll the fluted edge with a
wooden cocktail stick (toothpick) to
frill it. Attach to the neck with royal
icing. Stick the ice cream cornet hat
on with royal icing.

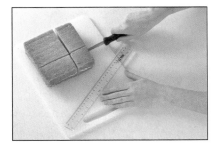

2 Split and fill the cake with
butter icing. Cut a 5 cm/2 in
strip from two sides of the cake to
create a 10 cm/4 in square, a
5 cm/2 in square and two rectangles.

5 Colour pieces of sugarpaste
black, green and red and roll
out. Cut out white and black shapes
for eyes, green spiky hair, red nose
and mouth and numbers for the sides
of the box. Attach with water.
Colour the remaining royal icing
yellow and pipe stars around the
edges of the cube and pompoms on
the hat, decorating with silver balls.

TELEPHONE CAKE

A great idea for a first or second birthday, as the telephone is an endless source of amusement for many toddlers.

INGREDIENTS

SERVES 8–10
2-egg quantity chocolate-flavour quick mix sponge
6 tbsp apricot jam, warmed and sieved
550 g/1 ¼lb sugarpaste (fondant) icing
1 quantity butter icing
red, blue, yellow and green food colourings
black liquorice ribbon

STORING
The iced cake can be kept in a cool, dry place for up to 3 days.

1 Preheat the oven to 180°C/350°F/ Gas 4. Lightly grease an 18 cm/ 7 in square cake tin, line with greaseproof (wax) paper and then grease the paper. Spoon the sponge mixture into the tin, level the top and bake in the centre of the oven for 35–40 minutes or until firm. Turn out on a wire rack and leave to cool.

2 Cut a 4 cm/1½ inch strip for the receiver. Cut the main cake in half. Cut one-quarter off the top half for the receiver rest.

3 Brush the centre of the main cake with apricot jam and reposition the top of the cake, leaving space for the receiver rest.

4 To shape the receiver rest, cut a 1 cm/½ in cross out of the centre then cut away the four corners. Brush the base with jam and position on the cake.

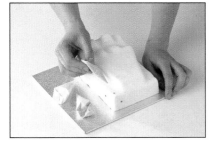

5 Brush the cake with jam. Roll out 350 g/12 oz of the sugar-paste (fondant) icing to a 30 cm/ 12 in square and use to cover the cake and place on a cake board. Divide the butter icing into three pieces. Colour one red, one blue and one yellow. Using piping bags with plain nozzles, pipe spots in all the colours evenly over the cake.

6 Colour 175 g/6 oz of the remaining sugarpaste green. Cut off about 25 g/1 oz, wrap and set aside. Brush the receiver with jam, roll out the large piece of sugarpaste and use to cover it. Position the receiver on the cake. Roll a small piece of green sugarpaste into a ball. Attach to the side of the receiver with water.

7 Roll out the remaining green sugarpaste; cut out a flowerpot shape. Dampen and stick to the front of the telephone. For the dial, colour the remaining sugarpaste red and roll out to a 7.5 cm/3 inch round. Use a tiny round cutter to stamp out the finger holes, and attach to the cake. Use butter cream to pipe the numbers.

8 To make the cord, twist the piece of liquorice tightly around a pencil and leave for 10 minutes. Remove the pencil, and press one end of the liquorice into the receiver and the other end into the back of the cake.

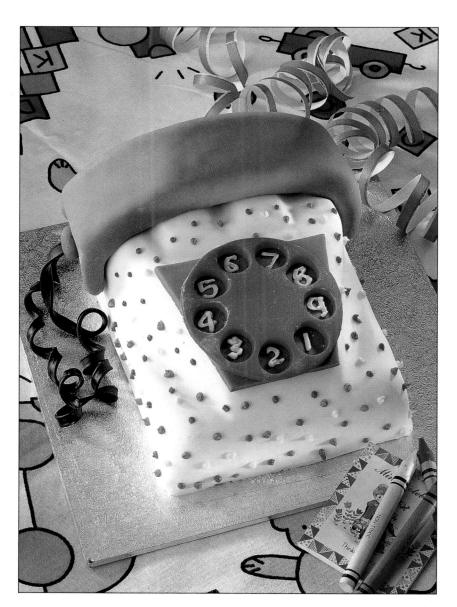

SAILING BOAT

For chocolate lovers, make a chocolate-flavoured sponge by substituting
50g/2 oz cocoa powder for the same quantity of flour.

INGREDIENTS

SERVES 12
4-egg quantity quick mix sponge
⅔ quantity butter icing
1 tbsp cocoa powder
4 large chocolate flakes
115 g/4 oz/⅙ quantity royal icing
blue food colouring
red and blue powder tints

1 Preheat the oven to 160°/325°F/ Gas 3. Grease a 20 cm/8 in square cake tin, line the base with greaseproof (wax) paper and grease the paper. Spoon in the cake mixture and bake for 50–60 minutes or until a skewer inserted in the centre of the cake comes out clean. Leave in the tin for 5 minutes, then turn out on to a wire rack. Remove the lining paper and cool.

2 Split and fill the cake with half the butter icing. Cut a 20 x 12 cm/8 x 5 in rectangle and trim to shape the hull of the boat.

4 Cut the sails and the flag from rice paper. Colour using powder tints. Wet the edges of the rice paper sails and stick on to a straw, holding in position until stuck. Insert the straw into the cake with the small sail at the front and the large one at the back. Stick the flag on to a cocktail stick (toothpick) and insert into the straw. Colour the royal icing blue and spread on the board in waves. Place ornaments on the boat.

3 Put the cake on a cake board. Mix the cocoa into the butter icing and spread over the boat. Split the flakes lengthways and press horizontally on the sides of the cake. Cut a flake in short lengths for the rudder and tiller and place at the stern. Sprinkle the crumbs on top.

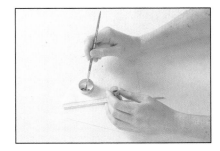

MOUSE IN BED

This cake is suitable for almost any age. The duvet and sheets may reflect the child's favourite colour. Make the mouse well ahead of time to allow it to dry.

INGREDIENTS

SERVES 16
4-egg quantity quick mix sponge
⅓ quantity butter icing
5 tbsp apricot jam, warmed and sieved
450 g/1 lb marzipan
675 g/1½ lb sugarpaste (fondant) icing
blue, brown and pink food colourings

1 Preheat the oven to 160°C/ 325°F/Gas 3. Grease a 20 cm/ 8 in square cake tin, line the base with greaseproof (wax) paper and grease the paper. Spoon in the cake mixture and bake in the oven for 50–60 minutes or until a skewer inserted in the centre comes out clean. Leave in the tin for 5 minutes, then turn out on to a wire rack. Remove lining paper and cool.

2 Split and fill the cake with butter icing. Cut 5 cm/2 in strip off one side and reserve. Place the cake on a cake board and brush with apricot jam. Cover with marzipan. Using the reserved cake, cut a pillow and cover with marzipan, pressing a hollow in the middle. Cut a body and legs and cover with marzipan. Leave to dry.

3 Cover the cake and pillow with white sugarpaste (fondant). Press a fork around the pillow edge to make a frill. Roll out 350 g/12 oz of the sugarpaste and cut into 7.5 cm/ 3 in wide strips. Dampen the bed edge and drape the valance around. To make the quilt, colour 75 g/3 oz sugarpaste blue and roll out to a square. Mark a diamond and flower pattern on the quilt. Put the pillow and body on top of the cake and cover with the quilt.

4 Roll out a little white sugarpaste and cut a strip for the sheet, mark along one length and place over the quilt, tucking in at the top. Colour 25 g/1 oz marzipan pink and make the head and paws. Put the head on the pillow and the paws over the edge of the sheet. Paint on features with food colouring.

PORCUPINE

*Melt-in-the mouth strips of flaky chocolate bars give this porcupine its
spiky coating. It's a fun cake for a children's or adults' party.*

INGREDIENTS

SERVES 15
*3-egg quantity chocolate-flavoured
quick mix sponge
2 quantities chocolate-flavoured
butter icing
50 g/2 oz white marzipan
cream, black, green, brown and red
food colourings
5–6 chocolate flake bars*

STORING
*Kept in a container in the refrigerator,
the cake will stay fresh for up to 3
days.*

3 Cut the flake bars into thin
strips and stick into the butter
icing to represent spikes.

1 Preheat the oven to 160°/325°F/
Gas 3. Grease and line the bases
of a 1 litre/½ pint/5 cup and a
600 ml/1 pt/2½ cup pudding bowl.
Spoon the cake mixture into both
bowls until two-thirds full. Bake in
the oven, allowing 55 minutes for the
large cake and 35–40 minutes for the
small cake. Turn out and cool. Take
the small cake and slice off a piece,
at an angle, from either side to create
a pointed nose for the porcupine.

4 Reserve a small portion of
marzipan. Divide the remainder
into four and colour black, green,
brown and cream. Shape the
marzipan as follows: cream to make
ears and feet, black and white for
eyes, and black for nose and claws.
Attach everything to the cake
as shown.

2 Place the large cake behind the
small one. Cut one of the cut-off
slices in half and position either side,
between the cakes, to fill in the gaps.
Place the other cut-off piece to fill in
the top, securing all with butter
icing. Spread the remaining icing over
the cake. Mark the face with a fork.

5 Shape the green and brown
marzipan into apples and stems.
Paint the apples with a little red
colouring and position next to the
porcupine.

MAGIC RABBIT

This cheery rabbit bursting from a top hat is the perfect centrepiece
for a magic theme party.

INGREDIENTS

SERVES 8–10
4-egg quantity quick mix sponge
⅔ quantity butter icing
115 g/4 oz royal icing
3 tbsp apricot jam, warmed and sieved
450 g/1 lb marzipan
675 g/1½ lb sugarpaste (fondant) icing,
coloured grey
225 g/8 oz marzipan, coloured pink
black and pink food colourings
silver balls

STORING
This cake will keep for 1 week, loosely
covered in foil in a cool, dry place.

1 Preheat the oven to 160°/325°F/ Gas 3. Grease 2 x 15 cm/6 in round cake tins, line the bases with greaseproof (wax) paper and grease the paper. Divide the cake mixture between the tins and bake in the oven for 35–45 minutes or until a skewer inserted in the centre comes out clean. Leave for 5 minutes, then turn out on to a wire rack. Remove the lining paper and cool. Split the cakes and then stack on top of one another, filling with the butter icing. Put on a board and brush with apricot jam.

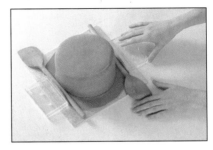

2 Cover with marzipan then with grey sugarpaste (fondant). Roll out the remaining sugarpaste to 20 cm/8 in round. Cut a 15 cm/6 in circle from the centre and put to one side. Lower the ring-shaped piece carefully over the cake. Fold up the sides and hold in place to dry.

3 Cut a cross in the centre of the grey circle, and place on the hat and curl the triangles over a spoon to shape. Smooth the join around the outside edge.

4 Using pink marzipan, shape the rabbit's head. Mark eyes, nose and mouth. Shape the ears and leave to dry overnight. Stick the rabbit in the centre of the hat with royal icing. Tie a ribbon round the hat. Pipe royal icing around the top and base and decorate with silver balls.

5 Colour the remaining royal icing black and pipe the eyes and mouth.

GHOST

This children's cake is really simple to make, yet very effective.

INGREDIENTS

*4-egg quantity orange-flavoured
quick mix sponge
900 g/2 lb sugarpaste (fondant) icing
black food colouring
1 quantity butter icing
cornflour (cornstarch), for dusting*

STORING

*The iced cake can be covered loosely
in foil and stored in a cool, dry place
for up to 2 weeks.*

1 Preheat the oven to 150°C/
300°F/Gas 2. Grease an 18 cm/
7 in square cake tin and line the base
with greased greaseproof (wax)
paper. Grease a 300 ml/½ pt/1¼ cup
pudding bowl and line the base with
greaseproof paper. Half-fill the bowl
with cake mixture and turn the
remainder into the cake tin. Bake the
bowl for 25 minutes and the tin for
1½ hours. Allow to cool. Then
colour 115 g/4 oz of the sugarpaste
(fondant) icing black and use to
cover the cake board.

2 Cut two small corners off the
large cake. Cut 2 larger wedges
off the other 2 corners. Stand the
large cake on the board. Halve the
larger cake trimmings and wedge
around the base of the cake.

3 Secure the small cake to the top
of the larger cake with a little of
the butter icing. Cover the cake with
the remaining butter icing. Roll out
the sugarpaste on a surface dusted
with cornflour (cornstarch) to a large
oval. Lay over the cake, letting the
icing fall into folds.

4 Gently smooth the icing over the
top half of the cake and trim
any excess at the base. Using black
food colouring and a fine paintbrush,
paint two oval eyes on to the head.

BALLERINA

*This cake requires patience and plenty of time for the decoration. The
tiny flowers were made with 5 mm/¼ in and 8 mm/⅓ in flower cutters with ejectors.*

INGREDIENTS

SERVES 8

3-egg quantity quick mix sponge
⅓ quantity butter icing
3 tbsp apricot jam, warmed and sieved
450 g/1 lb marzipan
450 g/1 lb sugarpaste (fondant) icing
*pink, yellow and green food
colourings*
115 g/4 oz/⅙ quantity royal icing

STORING

*This cake will keep for 1 week, loosely
covered in foil in a cool dry place.*

1 Preheat the oven to 160°F/325°F/
Gas 3. Grease a 20 cm/8 in
round cake tin, line the base with
greaseproof (wax) paper and grease
the paper. Spoon in the cake mixture
and bake for 45–55 minutes or until
a skewer inserted in the centre
comes out clean. Leave in the tin for
5 minutes then turn out on to a wire
rack. Remove the lining paper and
leave to cool. Split and fill the cake
with butter icing. Place on a board
and brush with apricot jam. Cover
with marzipan then white sugarpaste
(fondant). Leave to dry.

2 Divide the remaining sugarpaste
into 3; colour with flesh tones,
dark pink and pale pink. Cut out
flowers for the hoop and the head-
dress using pale pink sugarpaste.
Leave to dry.

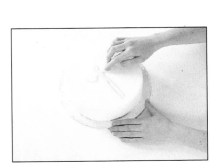

3 Using a template cut out the
body from flesh-coloured
sugarpaste and stick on the cake with
a little water. Then cut out a bodice
from the dark pink sugarpaste and
stick in place.

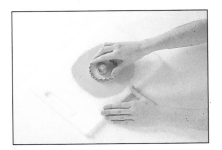

4 To make the tutu, roll out dark
pink sugarpaste and cut out a
fluted circle. Then cut out an inner
circle with a small, plain cutter.

5 Cut the ring into 4 and with
a cocktail stick (toothpick), roll
along the fluted edge to stretch and
frill it. Attach the frills to the waist
with a little water. Leave to dry
overnight.

6 With royal icing, pipe on a hoop and attach flowers to it. Colour a little royal icing green and pipe leaves in between. Paint on the face and hair. Stick tiny flowers around the head. Use pale pink sugarpaste for shoes and paint on ribbons. Pipe the flower centres on the hoop and head-dress using dark pink royal icing. Pipe white royal icing around the base of the cake and finish off with a ribbon.

BUMBLE BEE

This friendly bee is very effective, but quick and simple to construct. The edible sugar flowers may be brought ready-made, but these ones were made specially, and are very easy to make.

INGREDIENTS

SERVES 8–10
3-egg quantity quick mix sponge
⅓ quantity butter icing
3 tbsp apricot jam, warmed and sieved
350 g/12 oz marzipan
350 g/12 oz sugarpaste (fondant) icing,
coloured yellow
115 g/4 oz sugarpaste (fondant) icing,
coloured black
50 g/2 oz sugarpaste (fondant) icing
yellow, black, blue, red and green
food colourings
115 g/4 oz/⅙ quantity royal icing
50 g/2 oz/½ cup desiccated (shredded)
coconut

STORING

This cake will keep for 1 week loosely
covered in foil in a
cool, dry place.

1 Preheat the oven to 160°F/325°/ Gas 3. Grease a 20 cm/8 in round cake tin, line the base with greaseproof (wax) paper and grease the paper. Spoon in the cake mixture and bake for 45–55 minutes or until a skewer inserted in the centre comes out clean. Leave in the tin for 5 minutes, then turn out on to a wire rack. Remove the lining paper and allow to cool. Split and fill the cake with the butter icing.

3 Roll out the black sugarpaste and then cut out three strips 2.5 x 25cm/ 1 x 10 in and stick on the cake with a little water. Reserving a small piece of white sugarpaste, colour some blue, some yellow and the rest pink. Use to make white and blue eyes and a pink mouth and stick on cake with water. Cut out six 2.5 cm/1 in rounds from pink sugarpaste and stick small balls of yellow on each. Prick the centres with a cocktail stick (toothpick) and cut petals with a knife.

2 Cut the cake in half and stand upright together on a cake board. Trim to shape a head and tail. Brush with jam. Cover with marzipan then yellow sugarpaste.

4 Colour the coconut green. Cover the cake board with royal icing, sprinkle with coconut, and place the daisies on top. Bend 2 pipe cleaners in half and stick in the body for the wings. Cut a doily in half and use the pieces to cover the pipe cleaners.

NOAH'S ARK

This charming cake is decorated with small purchased animals, about
4 cm/1½ in high, available from cake decorating shops. Children will love
to take home 1 of the novelties, as a reminder of the party.

INGREDIENTS

SERVES 16

4-egg quantity quick mix sponge
⅓ quantity butter icing
6 tbsp apricot jam, warmed and sieved
450 g/1 lb marzipan
450 g/1 lb sugarpaste (fondant) icing,
coloured light brown
115 g/4 oz/⅙ quantity royal icing
yellow and blue food colourings
rice paper triangle
chocolate mint stick

STORING

This cake will keep for 1 week loosely
covered in foil in a cool, dry place.

1 Preheat the oven to 160°F/325°F/
Gas 3. Grease a 20 cm/8 in
square cake tin, line the base with
greaseproof (wax) paper and grease
the paper. Spoon in the cake mixture
and bake in the oven for 50–60
minutes or until a skewer inserted in
the centre comes out clean. Leave in
the tin for 5 minutes, then turn out
on to a wire rack. Remove the lining
paper and allow to cool. Split and
fill the cake with butter icing.

2 Cut a hull shape 20 x 13 cm/
8 x 5 in, and put on a board.
Cut a cabin, 10 x 6 cm/4 x 2½ in,
and a triangular roof. Sandwich
together with butter icing.

3 Brush the cake with jam, cover
with marzipan and then cover
the hull and cabin with light brown
sugarpaste (fondant). Place the cabin
and roof on the hull. Roll the brown
sugarpaste into a sausage, and attach
to edge of hull. Mark planks with
the back of a knife.

4 Colour half the royal icing
yellow and spread on the roof to
look like thatch. Colour the
remaining icing blue and spread on
the board to look like waves. Make
a flag with the rice paper and
chocolate stick and place on the cake
together with the purchased animals.

Quick Mix Sponge Cake

This is a quick-and-easy reliable recipe for making everyday cakes in various sizes, shapes and flavours.

Ingredients

2-EGG QUANTITY
115 g/4 oz/1 cup self-raising flour
1 tsp baking powder
115 g/4 oz/½ cup caster (superfine) sugar
115 g/4 oz/½ cup soft margarine
2 eggs

3-EGG QUANTITY
175 g/6 oz/1½ cup self-raising flour
1½ tsp baking powder
175 g/6 oz/¾ cup caster (superfine) sugar
175 g/6 oz/¾ cup soft margarine
3 eggs

4-EGG QUANTITY
225 g/8 oz/2 cup self-raising flour
2 tsp baking powder
225 g/8 oz/1 cup caster (superfine) sugar
225 g/8 oz/1 cup soft margarine
4 eggs

Storing and Freezing
The cake can be made up to 2 days in advance, wrapped in clear film (plastic wrap) or foil and stored in an airtight container. The cake can be frozen for up to 3 months.

1 Preheat the oven to 160°/325°F/ Gas 3. Prepare the tin according to the recipe.

2 Sift the flour and baking powder into a bowl. Add sugar, margarine and eggs. Mix together with a wooden spoon, then beat for 1–2 minutes until smooth and glossy.

3 Stir in chosen flavourings and beat until evenly blended.

4 Pour into the prepared tin, level the top and bake as required.

Flavourings

The following amounts are for a 2-egg quantity cake. Increase the suggested flavourings to suit the quantity being made.

CITRUS – 2 tsp finely grated orange, lemon or lime rind
CHOCOLATE – add 1 tbsp cocoa powder blended with 1 tbsp boiling water, or 26 g/1 oz/scant ¼ cup chocolate dots, melted
COFFEE – 2 tsp coffee granules blended with 1 tsp boiling water
NUTS – replace 25 g/1 oz/2 tbsp flour with finely ground nuts

Lining a Cake Tin

Lining tins is important so that the cakes come out of the tin without breaking or sticking to the base of the tin.

1 Place the tin on a piece of greaseproof (waxed) paper, draw around the base with a pencil and cut out the paper inside this line.

2 Grease the base and sides of the tin with melted lard or soft margarine and stick the piece of paper in neatly. Grease the paper. It is now ready for filling.

Rich Fruit Cake

This recipe makes a very moist rich cake suitable for any celebration.

Ingredients

Cake tin sizes	18 cm/7 in Square 20 cm/8 in Round	20 cm/8 in Square 23 cm/9 in Round	23 cm/9 in Square 25 cm/10 in Round	25 cm/10 in Square 28/11 in Round
Raisins	325 g/11 oz/ 2 cups	375 g/13 oz/ 2½ cups	425 g/15 oz/ 2⅔ cups	575 g/1¼ lb/ 3¾ cups
Sultanas (golden raisins)	225 g/6 oz/ 1½ cups	275 g/10 oz/ 1⅔ cups	350 g/12 oz/ 2¼ cups	475 g/1 lb 1 oz/ 3¼ cups
Currants	175 g/6 oz/ 1½ cup	225 g/8 oz/ 1¼ cups	275 g/10 oz/ 2 cups	400 g/14 oz/ 3 cups
Glacé (candied) cherries halved	150 g/5 oz/ 1 cup	175 g/6 oz/ 1 cup	200/7 oz/ 1⅓ cups	225 g/8 oz/ 1½ cups
Mixed (candied) peel	50 g/2 oz/ ⅓ cup	75 g/3 oz/ ½ cup	125 g/4 oz/ ¾ cup	175 g/ 6 oz/ 1 cup
Flaked almonds	50 g/2 oz/ ½ cup	75 g/3 oz/ ¾ cup	125 g/4 oz/ 1 cup	175 g/6 oz/ 1⅔ cups
Lemon rind, coarsely grated	10 ml/2 tsp/ 2 tsp	12 ml/2½ tsp/ 2½ tsp	15 ml/1 tbsp 1 tbsp	25 ml/1½ tbsp/ 1½ tbsp
Lemon juice	30 ml/2 tbsp/ 2 tbsp	40 ml/2½ tbsp/ 2½ tbsp	45 ml/3 tbsp/ 3 tbsp	60 ml/4 tbsp/ 4 tbsp
Brandy or sherry	45 ml/3 tbsp/ 3 tbsp	60 ml/4 tbsp/ 4 tbsp	75 ml/5 tbsp/ 5 tbsp	90 ml/6 tbsp/ 6 tbsp
Plain (all-purpose) flour	250 g/9 oz/ 2¼ cups	325 g/11 oz/ 3½ cups	400 g/14 oz/ 3½ cups	500 g/1 lb 2 oz/ 4½ cups
Mixed spice	12 ml/2½ tsp/ 2½ tsp	15 ml/1 tbsp/ 1 tbsp	18 ml/1¼ tbsp/ 1¼ tbsp	25 ml/1½ tbsp/ 1½ tbsp
Ground almonds	65g/2½ oz/ ⅔ cup	125 g/4 oz/ 1¼ cups	150 g/5 oz/ 1⅓ cups	225 g/8 oz/ 2¼ cups
Dark brown sugar	200 g/7 oz/ 1⅓ cups	250 g/9 oz/ 1⅔ cups	350 g/12 oz/ 2¼ cups	475 g/1 lb 1 oz/ 3⅓ cups
Butter, softened	200 g/7 oz/ 1 cup	250 g/9 oz/ 1¼ cups	350 g/12 oz/ 1½ cups	475 g/1 lb 1 oz/ 2¼ cups
Black treacle (or molasses)	25 ml/1½ tbsp/ 1½ tbsp	30 ml/2 tbsp/ 2 tbsp	40 ml/2½ tbsp/ 2½ tbsp	45 ml/3 tbsp/ 3 tbsp
Eggs	4	5	6	7
Approx. Cooking time	3–3½ hours	3¼–3¾ hours	3¾–4¼ hours	4–4½ hours

1 Into a large bowl place the raisins, sultanas (golden raisins), currants, glacé (candied) cherries, mixed (candied) peel, flaked almonds, lemon rind and juice, brandy or sherry. Mix all the ingredients together until well blended, then cover the bowl with cling film (plastic wrap). Leave overnight.

2 Preheat the oven to 140°/275°F/Gas 1 and grease and line a deep cake tin. Sift the flour and mixed spice into another bowl. Add the ground almonds, sugar, butter, treacle (or molasses) and eggs. Mix together with a wooden spoon, then beat for 1–2 minutes until smooth and glossy. Alternatively, beat for 1 minute using an electric mixer.

3 Gradually add mixed fruit and fold into cake mixture until all the fruit has been evenly blended.

4 Spoon the mixture into the prepared tin and spread evenly. Smooth the surface with the back of a metal spoon, making a slight depression in the centre.

5 Bake the cake in the centre of the oven following the chart cooking times as a guide. Test the cake to see if it is cooked 30 minutes before the end of the cooking time. The cake should feel firm, and when a fine skewer is inserted into the centre, it should come out quite clean. If the cake is not cooked, retest it at 15-minute intervals. Remove the cake from the oven and allow it to cool in the tin.

6 Turn the cake out of the tin but do not remove the lining paper as it helps to keep the moisture in. Spoon half the quantity of brandy or sherry used in each cake over the top of the cake and wrap in a double thickness of foil.

BUTTER ICING

This popular icing is made quickly with butter and icing (confectioner's) sugar

INGREDIENTS

Makes 359 g/12 oz
115 g/4 oz/½ cup unsalted butter, softened
225 g/8 oz/2 cups icing (confectioner's) sugar, sifted
2 tsp milk
1 tsp vanilla essence (extract)

FLAVOURINGS

CITRUS – replace milk and vanilla essence with orange, lemon or lime juice and 2 tsp finely grated orange, lemon or lime rind. Omit the rind if the icing is to be piped.
CHOCOLATE – 1 tbsp cocoa powder blended with 1 tbsp boiling water, cooled.
COFFEE – 1 tsp coffee granules blended with 1 tbsp boiling water, cooled.

1 Place the butter in a bowl. Using a wooden spoon or an electric mixer, beat until light and fluffy.

2 Stir in the icing (confectioner's) sugar, milk and vanilla essence (extract), and/or flavourings until evenly mixed, then beat well until light and smooth. Use as required.

HOMEMADE MARZIPAN

Marzipan is extremely versatile, it can be used as an attractive cake coating as well as a base.

INGREDIENTS

Makes 450 g/1 lb
225 g/8 oz/2¼ cups ground almonds
115 g/4 oz/½ cup caster (superfine) sugar
115 g/4 oz/¾ cup icing (confectioner's) sugar, sifted
1 tsp lemon juice
few drops almond essence (extract)
1 large egg, or 1 small egg white, beaten

1 Place the ground almonds and sugars into a bowl. Stir until evenly mixed.

2 Make a "well" in the centre and add the lemon juice, almond essence (extract) and enough egg or egg white to mix to a soft but firm dough, using a wooden spoon.

3 Lightly dust a surface with icing sugar and knead the marzipan until smooth and free from cracks.

4 Wrap in cling film (plastic wrap) or store in a polythene bag until required..

SUGARPASTE

Sugarpaste (fondant) icing is one of the most versatile of icings.

INGREDIENTS

Makes 575 g /1¼ lb
1 egg white
2 tbsp liquid glucose
2 tsp rosewater
450 g/1 lb/1½ cups icing (confectioner's) sugar, sifted
icing sugar to dust

STORING

Wrap the icing completely in clear film (plastic wrap), or store in a polythene bag with all the air excluded.

2 Knead together with the fingers until the mixture forms into a ball.

1 Place the egg white, liquid glucose and rosewater into a clean bowl. Mix together to break up the egg white. Add the icing (confectioner's) sugar and combine with a wooden spoon until the icing begins to bind together.

3 Place on a surface lightly dusted with icing (confectioner's) sugar and knead until smooth and free from cracks. If the icing is too soft to handle and is sticky, knead in some more sifted icing sugar until firm and pliable. If the sugarpaste should dry out and become hard, knead in a little boiled water until the icing is soft and pliable.

ROYAL ICING

Royal icing has gained a regal position in the world of icing

INGREDIENTS

Makes 675 g/1½ lb
3 egg whites
about 675 g/1½ lb/6 cups icing (confectioner's) sugar, sifted
1½ tsp glycerine
few drops lemon juice
colouring (optional)

STORING

Royal icing will keep for up to 3 days in an airtight container, stored in the refrigerator. Stir the icing well before using.

1 Put the egg whites in a bowl and stir lightly with a wooden spoon. Add the icing (confectioner's) sugar gradually in small quantities, beating well with a wooden spoon between each addition. Add sufficient icing sugar to make a smooth, shiny icing with the consistency of very stiff meringue.

2 Beat in the glycerine, lemon juice and food colouring, if using. Cover the surface with a piece of damp clear film (plastic wrap) so the icing does not dry out. If possible, leave to stand for 1 hour. Before using, stir the icing to burst any air bubbles.

INDEX